500

To Steve

ANDERSON

BEST

WISHES

Charlie Plumb

THE LAST DOMINO?

News Reporter: "Mr. President, would you mind commenting on the strategic importance of Indochina to the Free World? . . ."

President Dwight D. Eisenhower: "Finally you have. . .what you would call the 'falling domino' principle. You have a row of dominos set up, you knock over the first one, and what will happen to the last one is the certainty that it will go over very quickly."

—Press Conference, April 7, 1954.

A POW LOOKS AHEAD

THE LAST DOMINO?

BY CHARLIE PLUMB

INDEPENDENCE PRESS

Library of Congress Cataloging in Publication Data

Plumb, Charlie.
  The last domino?

    1. Vietnamese Conflict, 1961-1975—United States.
I. Title.
DS558.2.P58   959.704'3373   75-20344
ISBN 0-8309-0150-7

                Printed in the United States of America
                                by
Independence Press, Drawer HH, Independence, Missouri 64055

TABLE OF CONTENTS

CHAPTER 1

WELCOME HOME

Peace. I've never seen a land more at peace. Timeless rock and water form a carpet stretching from horizon to horizon in the north country above the Arctic circle. The only visible change in season is the green of the tundra in summer and the white of the winter snow.

I looked from the copilot seat of the Twin Beech. The silver spinner on the starboard prop flickered like an old-time movie. As it twinkled, it reflected the brilliant blue above us and the mosaic of lakes below.

The bush pilot draped his right hand over the throttles and held an aeronautical chart against the yoke with his left. One finger carefully crawled along from lake to lake as the "bug smasher" droned away.

"Not too many landmarks up here," I suggested, just to start the conversation.

"Nope," he answered through a thick black beard. "A guy can fly for days in this country and never see a thing that's been touched by anyone." And his finger kept inching along the chart.

The flight was recreational. The cargo: fishermen. The destination: Tree River, Northwest Territories, the Arctic.

The Twin Beech had made this trip before. Her pontoons had plied the crystal waters of Great Bear Lake, the salt water of the Arctic Ocean, and the fresh water of a thousand different lakes between. She had hauled tons of cargo into the bush for trappers and fishermen. And she had winged back to civilization with the frozen bodies of hunters who had stayed too long.

But this cargo was a happy one. World-renowned fisherman Harold Ensley had offered me a welcome-home gift of this trip. Our whole party had come to the Arctic to catch some fish, and we weren't leaving till we tied into the big ones.

"There's the camp." The bush pilot lifted his right arm off the throttles and extended his red plaid sleeve forward. I nodded. I could barely see several tiny dots—the tents we would soon call home. The only distinguishing features were their oblong shapes.

"First square corners I've seen since we took off," I mused. The pilot refolded his chart, leaned to the left in his seat, and wedged the map under his right leg.

"Want to take her in?" He smiled for the first time.

"No, I'll leave that to you," I answered. He sat up a descent into the mouth of Tree River and, with the care of a new mother putting her sleeping baby into the crib, greased the Twin Beech onto the water.

We wasted no extra minutes unloading the fishing equipment onto a floating dock. The sun was already low on the mountains, and we weren't sure just how much light was left.

We tossed our packs and most of our fishing gear into a tent and pushed off for the river.

Serenity must have originated in the north country. As I stood atop a rock ledge, high above the ambling river, I was inundated with silence. No cars, no planes, no clanking cell doors or jingle of prison keys. I felt the whole world must be standing in awe of this peace. And how far, how very far away was Vietnam and the Indochina war.

I sat down on a clump of spongy tundra and

felt alone for the first time since my release from the POW prison in Hanoi. Suddenly I became pensive—as I had done so many times in prison—pondering the whys and wherefores of life itself. Somehow it seemed logical to sit up there on top of the world listening to the only audible noise—my own heartbeat—and challenge myself for some answers.

How did we ever get into that war anyway? What was the fighting for and...was it worth it? And now that it was all over, were all those lives lost in vain? Was it really necessary to have peace with honor? What would happen to Indochina and to America? Each question hurt a little when I asked it...and the hurt increased as I tried to answer.

Our homecoming as POWs had been the most wonderful moment of our lives, and we were both humble and grateful—to God and our nation—for our return. But we were first and foremost military professionals, determined to succeed. And we were very serious about the goals for which we'd fought and very disappointed in the errors which had been made. We all knew it was a gamble before we left for Vietnam, and we were ready to take chances. Now that the war was finally over and the Communists had infiltrated South Vietnam, we didn't want to admit we'd lost. As with many other inevitables, it hurt a little for us to prove the truth to ourselves.

There was no question that the withdrawal from Vietnam and the repatriation of the POWs had been an ill-fated attempt to close out the file marked "Indochina."

Washington held its breath with the hope that the tragic events of the decade were localized in Vietnam; that the blunders we made there would not affect our worldwide prestige; and that surrounding neutral and pro-American countries would understand the internal disease of the Vietnamese government and would be careful not to "catch cold."

We assumed that our role as an international gendarme was only some political writer's simile, and that the average cone-hatted peasant looked upon the bearded Uncle Sam as more of a Madison Avenue billboard figure than a viable protector of his private freedoms. Or maybe the provincial peasant didn't look upon Uncle Sam at all but was interested only in the source of his next bowl of rice. And in that case, perhaps we had an even heavier responsibility, called the white man's burden, to protect these poor under-developed folk from the things they didn't know would hurt them.

Anyway, we thought Hanoi would surely stop to digest South Vietnam before continuing the quest to gather all of the peninsula under one red flag. And even if it proceeded at top speed, North Vietnam could never move so fast as to topple the Indochina dominoes before we could step in with a well-placed big toe and halt the fall of the next domino in the line.

Washington held its breath for two years. And just about the time we gave a sigh of relief, our nation was again reminded of Indochina. Those chronic pains were renewed and we were awakened by some stark realities—realities which we tried to rationalize. And when they wouldn't fit rational formulas, we tried to ignore them.

The North Vietnamese and their guerrillas, the Viet Cong, had started their inexorable move south. The American trained and equipped South Vietnamese armies (ARVN) had looked once toward the enemy and once away from the enemy. Their first glance showed them a well trained, heavily armed military force. Their second glance showed them the beaten trail the Americans took back home. The ARVNs turned south and ran.

Much to our dismay our allies not only gave freely the key positions bought by American blood but left behind all the U.S.-made weapons we had given them. The Communist momentum continued to build until even Saigon was taken.

After the shock of their freely forfeiting the land we had spent years and lives and billions of dollars to acquire, we had only one follow-up question: "Where did we go wrong?"

To begin with, the Vietnam struggle was not a local war. The fighting had been somewhat contained in a geographical area, but the world watched. And the leaders of every under-developed nation felt a psychological transfer into Saigon's presidential palace when the Republic of South Vietnam domino began to teeter and the United States stood by with arms folded.

The closer the nation to the blast, the greater the shock. Countries like Laos and Thailand were ready for the collapse of Vietnam. Cambodia had its reaction already rehearsed. Nations on the outskirts like India and Malaysia took a little longer look. Their bread and butter were at stake.

———

The evolution of the foreign aid program of both the Communist and free world had come on like wheat after a spring rain. Our increased competition in this "aid race" had caused a great dependency by members of the Third World on the donor nations. This dependency put new emphasis on the "butter up" diplomacy of small nations. India and Malaysia no longer look upon redirecting their allegiance as "catching cold" but as switching doctors.

The role of the United States and its allies as world protectors of freedom is not just a fictitious simile drafted by a journalist. The million refugees who fled Communist rule as the North Vietnamese came south will verify that. The tens of thousands who set out to sea on anything that would float, desperately seeking rescue by American ships, weren't political scientists or international strategists and probably never knew the U.S. as an "international gendarme." They were simple people who heard the U.S. had been in the business of protecting personal freedoms for two hundred years, and that was impetus enough for them to leave their land and homes. The provincial peasant *is* primarily interested in the source of his next bowl of rice, but he looks to the free world to help him find it and protect him while he eats it.

Hanoi has always been slow to react, as if every move in the chess game has been thought out with painstaking deliberation. The North Vietnamese had never during the decade of the war been quick to take the initiative. Why should they suddenly sweep through the south and send guerrilla insurgents into neighboring countries?

Very simply—because their opposition had disappeared.

Any well-trained guerrilla meters his action according to the strength and mobility of his opponent. Throughout the Vietnam War the North Vietnamese Army (NVA) found resistance at every turn. Our military reaction was only the most obvious. The political staying power we demonstrated was even more formidable. Our tenacity, though less tangible input, was just as important as the howitzer count in directing the response of General Giap's army.

As aid was cut off by the U.S. Congress the morale of the ARVNs sank and the Communists began to move. Finding no military resistance and no political staying power behind their adversary, our own American-built tanks tracked down Highway 1 with red flags fluttering behind.

"Hey, Plumber...you gonna sit there all day?" Harold Ensley broke my train of thought. "Get down here and I'll show you how to catch the big uns."

CHAPTER 2

THE END
OF THE WAR

Johnny came marching home all right. Like in any other war in U.S. history, he came marching...only this time it was in the back door. But that wasn't too important to Johnny —he never wanted to be a hero anyway; he just wanted to get home and quit marching.

Johnny's dad was glad to see him, but it was tough for any father to slap his boy on the back and ask him how it felt not to be the victor. "Sure was different in the real war," he'd say. "If we'd had any sense we'd have got the whole thing over with...just like we did in Japan." Bitterness would creep into his eyes when he thought of his boy and the futility of the fight. "At least we had a purpose in World War II," he'd recall.

17

Johnny's little brother was glad to see him and wanted to hear about the excitement of fighting in a foreign country with a gun that would blow up anything, and riding a helicopter and chasing commies. "I just hope there's a war when I grow up!" was his major concern.

Johnny's mother was glad to see her son. She had never understood war but the Bible predicted a lot of it and she surely believed in the Bible. In fact she knew his safe return was an answer to her prayers. She had continued to pray that the strain of war wouldn't change "my John John."

Johnny's president was glad to see him. The war had done nothing for his administration but rip it apart. He had given up long ago on a military victory and had been looking only for an honorable peace. Since Johnny had been eleven, three different presidents had been looking for an honorable peace.

Peace with honor was important for all of us, just because of the makeup of our nation. Any nation can be described by more specific data than dotted lines on a map. Our self-identity as the United States includes a sizable element of pride: pride in our workmanship, pride in our living standard, pride in our word and deed. If that cohesive element of self-esteem ever fails to bind us together as a nation, those dotted lines will serve no more use than a reminder of a pretty design we used to call America.

And hand in hand with our pride goes a vital commitment to keep that pride alive. Those brave presidents were ready to sacrifice their own prestige to save the prestige of Americans. They knew that to surrender self-esteem was to scrap America.

My 2,103 days of imprisonment in North Vietnam were characterized by anxiety, fear, and terror. But I was never more horrified than the day our captors read to us George McGovern's platform for president and his offer to "crawl on his knees to Hanoi" in order to bring us home. We would rather have stayed in Vietnam than to have come home broken, worthless men.

So peace with honor and pride was important. And Mr. Nixon did well in ending our part of the Vietnam War gracefully.

Even so, few were happy. The doves had not accomplished their objectives. The hawks had been restrained from the beginning. And no one could point with pride at a list of liberties purchased by Uncle Sam with his seemingly unlimited supply of sons and dollars.

Two consolations were evident as the peace treaty was signed in January 1973: (1) the POWs were coming home; and (2) the government in

Saigon was not Communist. It was tough to find anything more to be glad about—for hawk or dove.

We war prisoners were indeed coming home, but not without a few scars. We had been made into such veteran poker chips our plastic coating was wearing thin. And even with all that action we still weren't contributing much. We were eventually allowed to become such a detriment to U.S. strategists that I'm sure they would have preferred to have taken us out of the game...but it was too late for that. Never before in the history of war have so few seemed so important to so many. And never before has a war been fought where such high dollar values were placed on human life.

It was all high-pressure playing, and the ante went up with each new card. The game was called five-card intimidation, and with satellite speed the U.S. and Hanoi launched verbal accusations about the inhumane treatment and the tiger cages and the torturous crimes being perpetrated by the other side. Lenient and humane treatment was the watchword as the body count kept climbing.

Meanwhile in the States there was a new vogue. "Bring home the POWs" became the rally banner when sophisticated Americans would not accept more traditional clichés such as "Remember the Maine" and "Hurray, Hurray for Tonkin Bay."

And it worked. Increased interest by Americans, the VIVA bracelet campaign, the letters from school children, the prayers from churches all combined to show Hanoi we were valuable people, and our lot as POWs improved. For that we were most grateful, but we were also frustrated; we wished the personal concern and fine support for us could have been extended to the administration and its commitment to our ally and the war cause.

As Americans became united in concern for us our treatment got better. Our food improved in quality and quantity. We were allowed outside our cells a few minutes each day. We were no longer forced to bow each time we wanted some drinking water. And the torture stopped for the most part. Our captors even gave us better washing facilities. But in the eyes of our negotiators at Paris that extra sliver of lye soap must have seemed a small price to pay for the great bargaining leverage the North Vietnamese gained. Our position was precarious, and we didn't appreciate our infamy any more than Washington did. Like it or not, we were still chips in the great showdown game.

And poor Saigon...poor war-torn, corrupt Saigon...at least it was free!

Every morning for months after my repatriation I feared the headlines in the daily newspaper. Just as the tide slowly surges up the red river engulfing millions of hectars of mud, the North Vietnamese Army would sweep through the south, I was convinced, as soon as the last GI had stepped onto the last C-5A. But it didn't happen. And I was relieved.

As Vietnam slid from today into yesterday, I gained the false confidence that perhaps we had trained a crack military unit in the South. And perhaps General No Dien Giap really was afraid his southern adversary would give his VC boys a bloody nose and a shove back north. Maybe the RVN's could hold on like the ROKs (Republic of Korea).

At the end of the Korean conflict and for several years after the peace settlement, the United States spent a good deal of time and money whipping the Republic of Korea military into a formidable force. It had taken a ragtag, lazy, undisciplined gang and built an army that could handle the dragon from the north.

Had we done the same thing in Vietnam? The Hanoi dragon didn't seem to be moving. Maybe it was dead!

Well, the dragon wasn't dead at all. It wasn't even sleeping. Hanoi's leaders had their eyes carefully focused on Capitol Hill. Every move that a congressman or senator made was another input to the strategical mechanism that controlled their "go" button.

The '74 Congressional elections in the U.S. pleased the Communist North Vietnamese, but they were still hesitant to take the big step. The timing was not quite right. Then the young, newly elected U.S. senators and representatives began to admire their own muscle. They had witnessed a "president's war" for ten years and felt it was time for the legislators to advise and dissent. And the same valve that Congress closed to stop aid to Indochina opened to send the North Vietnamese Army down Highway 1.

CHAPTER 3

SENTIMENT

"Thanks for your concern" was the mimeographed letterhead I used to respond to thousands of letters from around the world saying, "Welcome home, Charlie."

As I took those first giant steps on U.S. soil I found hundreds of wonderful friends with silver bracelets bearing my name. They really were concerned. But my mind could not help wandering back to those dark days of 1968 when the Paris talks had been stymied for the shape of a table—and no one seemed to care. As a dedicated military man I was destined to follow the command of the popular voice of my country. In 1968 that popular voice of the silent majority seemed ever so faint.

But not in 1973! Americans were vitally interested. Everyone wanted to know the POW story . . . and I wanted to tell them. But I wanted something in return. I wanted their reaction.

I began a series of speeches around the nation and the world. During my first six months of freedom I made nearly two hundred public appearances. And in return I gained a feel for public attitude toward me, the outcome of the war, and Americanism in general.

We repatriated POWs had become the sigh of relief of every American. A ticker tape parade would have been a better symbol. But we were all that was available, and that was enough to establish a sense of finality in the minds of most Americans. A finality to the frustrations of a too-long war. A finality to the humiliation of a stalemate. A finality to the nagging headache of unfinished international business.

As I have traveled several hundred thousand miles across this country as an ex-POW I have found that people react to me as if I were the end of the war personified. I meet joy and happiness from those who counted the days as I did until the peace treaty was finally signed. I see melancholy and tears from those who lost so much in the war. I find reluctance to speak by some who cannot communicate their feelings—but who come to shake the hand of a survivor. But of the more than one million Americans I've spoken to I have yet to encounter the slightest evidence of animosity or malice.

Students who were ready in 1970 to go to any extreme to belittle this country and blaspheme the military and all it stands for cautiously approach me with a certain awe of wonderment. They see me as a living ghost, a strange image they had fixed in their minds since the fourth grade but didn't believe really existed.

Then they hear the POW story—a testimony of faith, commitment, and pride. This seems to amaze them even more. "How can a man who has been through all that escape with anything other than bitterness?" they ask me.

"You gotta believe," I tell them. "It wasn't all that difficult."

Students or adults, rich or poor—all respond to my account. Often this is quite emotional. Sometimes I can offer an outlet for frustration or sympathy.

Many adults approach me with a hint of guilt and sorrow. I try to keep the conversation light, but in some cases it's obvious that a certain amount of company in misery is needed. And there's seldom a communication problem. We all shared the frustrations of watching that tiny light at the end of the tunnel as it got brighter, then dimmer, then brighter again.

"What could we have done?" is the question asked most frequently by adults. I tell them that I don't know any plan for serving our country, but once we're accustomed to caring then half the battle is won.

At one high school assembly where I spoke the response was especially warm. I shook the hands of several students in the small midwestern town, autographed their notebooks, and walked toward the door with the principal. As I approached the edge of the gymnasium bleachers an overall-clad, middle-aged man pulled himself to his feet and stepped toward me. His face tallied years of abuse from sun and sweat and wind. His hands were gnarled and creased. His limp told me he too had made a sacrifice. And his plaid shirt had felt more than once the tender fingers of a seamstress.

He spoke softly. "I'm sorry. I'm sorry but there was nothin' I could do. I wanted to...but I didn't know how." His brow furrowed with the struggle to hold back tears as he placed a quarter in the palm of my hand.

"This ain't much but I hope..." and he turned away without finishing the sentence. The pain had been too great.

The response of young adults has been

enthusiastic. In New York City a young lady reporter, unencumbered by her anti-war views, insisted on treating me to an evening on the town.

As the date began she had little empathy with me, but as I told her of my experiences and my feelings of commitment to duty, she suddenly seemed to realize why she had asked me out—not to entertain or woo but to soothe her own feelings of guilt. After that, nothing was too good for me. The evening ended with an argument in a restaurant at the top of a luxurious hotel: my escort insisting that the maitre d' give us the window table because "We owe it to the men who have suffered more than we."

Foreign audiences have been sympathetic also. I traveled to Israel shortly after my repatriation. I saw the Holy Land and Tel Aviv. I toured the Golan Heights two weeks before war broke out again. In a personal meeting with me Golda Meir expressed amazement that I had been in prison during her famous six-day war in 1967 and was not even aware of that great victory until two years after the fact.

Israelis seemed to identify with the South Vietnamese. Both were engaged in a great struggle and were proud to have the greatest power on earth on their side. And both knew they would win.

On the streets of Jerusalem I met a teen-age girl in military uniform. I started a conversation by asking about the silver band on her wrist. It looked identical to the POW bracelets worn by over a million Americans.

"Yes," she said in carefully metered English, "this is the name of a Jewish POW in Russia." Looking at me with piercing eyes she said, "We wore the names of American POWs until we brought them home. Now we are fighting for the repatriation of the prisoners held by the Russian communists."

The Spanish were not so intent. The flamenco guitarist Carlos Montoya invited me to his home in Madrid and had his private craftsman construct a guitar for me. (I had met Carlos in Miami and had explained how in prison I had fashioned a piece of bamboo into a guitar neck and practiced chord positions on the silent fingerboard. He was astounded at American ingenuity.) His lovely wife, who was educated in America, translated for him. "Carlos knows of the Vietnam tragedy and is saddened by your experience."

The militant Germans seemed to back the U.S. all the way. On the other hand, Canadians couldn't see our purpose for being in Vietnam. In Winnipeg I talked frankly with a CBC TV newsman about the draft dodgers. "I've known dozens of them," he said through a thick black beard. "Some are sincere. Some are afraid. Some are bloody beggars."

Overall Canadian opinion, he told me, was that the United States should never have become involved in Vietnam. "We Canadians don't go around picking fights. We don't want to be known as the world bully."

"I don't consider my country the world bully," I answered politely. "But you're sorely mistaken if you think freedom comes for free. Constant vigilance and occasional military action is necessary to prove our commitment to world peace and freedom."

With that my host asked me my opinion of draft dodgers.

"I feel no bitterness," I said. "For them leaving the States might have been the right thing to do. If I felt subjugated in America I'd want to move too. So they put their money down and they took their chance. They had full knowledge of possible repercussions. They went anyway. But now the war is over and many deserters want to come home. I strongly feel that those men have denounced America and her people. And until they can prove that they're worthy of the name

American, then I can't be proud to share that name with them."

I think President Ford had the right idea: make them earn their way home by doing something to contribute to society. It doesn't seem unreasonable to me to ask a man who slapped you in the face for an apology...especially if you're about to give him one of the greatest of gifts—American citizenship.

The scope of sentiment at home and around the world was broad. There seemed only one common denominator: everyone was concerned. In that I took consolation.

CHAPTER 4

DOMINO ONE
VIETNAM

Communist countries have an interesting way of updating their history books. Whenever a new reform measure is implemented, or a past hero is defrocked, the government recalls the "reactionary" information and puts in its place a new "time-honored" legend. This technique offers to the serious student of history an automatic credibility gap. But, willing to accept totalitarian accuracy, the researcher is aided by the obvious absence of conflicting accounts.

Many viewpoints of Ho Chi Minh have been set in type—but only one in North Vietnam. To the average peasant Uncle Ho is George Washington, John Wayne, and Jesus Christ all in one olive drab tunic. They write songs, draw pictures, compose poetry, light candles, plant trees, and drink *nuoc maum* all in the name of their great leader. He represents everything that is good.

According to the Hanoi press he was native born and educated, then went to sea—first as a line handler, then as the ship's cook. In his travels around the world he found himself in many ports of many French colonies.

In one episode Ho the cook came topside just as his French liner was pulling into an African colonial port. The natives came in boats and rafts as the bourgeois tossed francs into the water. Young Ho Chi Minh cried as he watched the Africans belittle themselves before their white landlords. He cried because of the empathy he felt for the Africans who were subjugated in much the same way as his own people.

Communist books point out how heartbroken Ho was to see such exploitation, and he decided to change all that. He joined the forces of colonized Vietnamese determined to change their own destiny.

He fought his first battles on podiums in Paris—to no avail. The French were too content with their rubber, tin, and rice imports from their Southeast Asian colonies to consider giving Vietnam autonomy.

Ho traveled the trail of the Troung Son

mountain range with little more than his bag of rice and a walking stick. His rubber-tire sandals stirred up dust while his charisma stirred up dissent.

Though response among the population was overwhelming, Ho Chi Minh didn't have the hardware to launch a military uprising. Then came his big break—World War II. With sights set much higher than on a small backward country the Japanese fought the French for Indochina in the early 1940's.

The North Vietnamese were committed to fight for the French at first but as the Japanese gained the upper hand, Ho and his Viet Minh went underground with their activities, waiting for the war to end and hoping the Japanese would lose. The Japanese did just that and were forced to move out of Vietnam and Indochina.

On August 3, 1945, Ho Chi Minh grasped the opportunity to declare independence from Japan, France, and whoever else might be listening to his strong voice on his weak shortwave transmitter: *Alea jacta est* (The die is cast)!

The French, claiming victory, wanted their colony back. The Japanese, being defeated, were willing to give it to them and go home. The Americans, being shortsighted, acquiesced.

Meanwhile Ho's budding young nation needed

support—financial, political, and military—and he wasn't too choosy about who he tapped. Since he had visited the United States, he decided to ask us for assistance. But due to our pseudo obligation to our pseudo ally, we chose to honor the French as the rightful rulers of Vietnam.

If only the foresight of Marshall and Truman could have been focused on what we now call the inevitable, perhaps thousands of lives could have been spared and a friendly—or at least neutral—nation would have emerged on the eastern coast of Indochina. But we didn't help the benevolent dictator, and the French went back to reestablish their influence. They spent millions of francs, thousands of lives, and nine years before they finally admitted they could no longer maintain control of a people by propping up an unpopular government. America wasn't watching.

We demonstrated our aloofness by supporting the remnants of the French Legion, some mercenaries, and a million refugees in search of a better way of life. They didn't know it then but those Vietnamese peasants were starting a long journey. Many of the same bewildered waifs we saw in photos climbing aboard the American landing craft heading south in '54 were boarding Boeing 747s heading east in '75.

36

Ho's victory at Dien Ben Phu and the subsequent division of Vietnam at the seventeenth parallel didn't solve the problem. The North Vietnamese stepped up their infiltration of the south, setting up an elaborate network of communication and transportation. Their guerrilla warfare—organized, supported, and led from the north yet fought below the demilitarized zone (seventeenth parallel)—was a method which would harass Saigon for twenty years.

The new Republic of Vietnam in the south was having enough problems of its own. Ngo Dinh Diem had declared that land mass independent and established himself as president. Diem was a harsh ruler but had more grass roots support and a better underground system than any other leader of that country had ever had or has had since. But he didn't keep his finger on the pulse of the people. Underestimating the power of the Buddhists, he shunned their demands. A heated conflict arose, and the Communists provided the catalyst. Diem was killed in a military coup in 1963.

During the next two years there were many power grabs and changing regimes in Saigon. Nguyen Van Thieu finally settled the government in 1967, somewhat unified the country, and appeased the U.S. in preparation for a full-scale war. But he was never in complete control and never had the true interest of freedom of his people in mind. His incentive, like that of other leaders we've supported, was primarily to improve his personal life-style and solidify his position of power through U.S. aid.

It is all too easy in retrospect to say we went to the derby and put our money on the wrong horse. (That observation is so obvious and so trite I hesitate to make it.) But we didn't learn—race after race after race.

CHAPTER 5

DOMINO TWO
CAMBODIA

A living Buddha—that's how I always remembered Prince Norodom Sihanouk. His rotund figure complemented that cunning grin to make him appear to be the final authority on just about everything. But like his next-door neighbor Ho Chi Minh he was a charismatic leader, loved and respected by the majority of his subjects. Unlike Vietnam's revolutionary leader, however, the prince was content to wait his turn for independence, thereby avoiding a great deal of bloodshed and destruction in his beautiful country. He did this by carefully riding the political fence. Even so, the history of Cambodia follows that of Vietnam and the other Indo-chinese countries.

Under a French protectorate from 1863, Cambodia was identified primarily by its Khmer language and ancient Buddhist temples. The French domination was strong then, but Cambodia never offered the natural resources and the accessibility of the eastern coastal real estate and thus was allowed to accept a secondary role when the French grip on Indochina began to weaken.

Sihanouk loved it. He gloated as the French were tossed out by the Japanese, who were in turn defeated by the United States. With amazing dexterity the round man tippy-toed along the international tightwire.

When the ashes of World War II were finally cold, Prince Norodom promulgated his own constitution—still within the French union. Again he took a backseat to the revolutionist Ho Chi Minh and sat on his throne with lips sealed—fangs withdrawn.

When the time was right, as the tattered French troops were being forgotten in Paris just seven months before Dien Ben Phu, the prince (now king) declared Cambodia's independence.

In years following, this Asian country continued to maintain neutrality and tried to be everybody's friend. It leaned toward the Communist block on several occasions but was clearly no satellite for China or Russia. Then came the Vietnam War. This time Cambodia was forced to become involved. In 1965 the Viet Cong were blatantly using the jungle border area to launch and recover attacks on populated areas of South Vietnam.

Sihanouk could in no way stop this action. His army was meager, ill-equipped, and lacked experience. Anyway, it was against his policy of peace and neutrality. But in the U.S. we could not accept Cambodia as a neutral when the enemy was storing fresh troops and tons of ammuniton there. We forced the hand of the king (now chief of state) in hopes he would get off his tightrope and hop on our bandwagon. Mistake!

Norodom Sihanouk reacted violently by cutting off all diplomatic relations with us and turning to the Communists for help. They came... and considered our broken friendship a major victory. Again this was not the result of their good judgment but rather our lack of foresight.

"But since he has shown his true colors," reasoned the naïve American strategists, "the Red Cambodian can't possibly be popular with his people. The country is ripe for a U.S.-engineered coup d'etat." And in March of 1970 it came.

That spring I was in a small prison cell in a POW jail near Hanoi. The food was rotten, the treatment worse, and the "squawk box" could be neither controlled nor ignored as it blared without end:

> The U.S.S. *Columbia Eagle* has mutinied. Anti-war American sailors have taken control of the freighter and have brought their shipload of arms and munitions into Sihanoukville, port city of Cambodia. These United States sailors have handed over large quantities of war supplies to Vietnamese freedom fighters. Sure and certain victory for the oppressed people in Indochina is near.

We were appalled that the North Vietnamese could even think of mutiny on an American ship. But the headlines continued throughout the week: "American Sailors Support National Liberation Front."

At the end of the week, however, another account of the incident was given:

> A clique of traitors, henchmen of U.S. imperialist aggressors and puppets of the Nixon regime, have sneaked into Cambodia's capital city, Phnom Penh, and in a coup d'etat have illegally taken control of the government. FUNK

fighters [Fighters of the United National Kingdom] tried desperately to retake the capital city and to re-establish the proper authority of Prince Norodom Sihanouk. They were unable to defend the city because imperialist aggressors had utilized a huge cache of weapons secretly smuggled in from a freighter called the U.S.S. *Columbia Eagle.*

We were ecstatic. We had never seen such a backfire on Communist propaganda. The coup had in fact taken place. While Sihanouk was out of the country, Lt. Gen. Lon Nol, the premier of the government, had taken control. His clout with the military officers and brashness with congress had allowed him to take the place of Norodom Sihanouk. But he didn't have the hearts of the Khmer people. And that made him another U.S. liability.

CHAPTER 6

DOMINO THREE
LAOS

The single most impressive thing about Laos is its flag. Three stately elephants all balanced on an imperial pedestal epitomize the character of the country. Laos is a nation of princes and peasants.

Laos was the "outback" section of the French Indochinese peninsula. Cambodia and Vietnam were the fair-haired children of the French as those two countries were more accessible and thus easier to exploit. They both had good ports so the French merchantmen could haul away tons of coal, copper, and rice. Landlocked Laos offered little attraction other than a few more hectars of jungle the French could call a colony.

As in the cases of its two neighbors, Vietnam and Cambodia, Laos found nationalistic fever spreading rampantly in the forties. Knowing that the French placed a much higher value on the other pieces of the Indochina pie, the king of Laos felt safe in declaring the independence of his country shortly after World War II. His army was ill-trained and ill-equipped and would have been no match for the French Legion, but the French had bigger problems over more valuable real estate and decided to let Laos go without a fight. The two parties signed a treaty in 1949 giving Laos independence.

The master plan was for Laos to remain neutral, but the Communist Pathet Lao Army working south from the China border wanted to exercise its power and control. Unfortunately it had the best equipped troops around. Prince Souphanouvong, leader of the Pathet Lao, tried his best to wedge his way into the Laotian parliament, but the neutral and right-wing factions of the government wanted no part of the prince or his Communist army. And in no way were the legitimate leaders going to allow an integration of this army with their own Royalist troops. Bloody fighting ensued.

The Soviets supplied most of the bullets and the North Vietnamese supplied some of the bodies as the red insurgency spread south.

In 1962 a peace treaty was signed in Geneva,

and Laos again had a clean slate but a coalition government that was doomed from the beginning.

Only two years later the Pathet Lao, again inspired by Ho Chi Minh and the Communist North, took to the hills and started guerrilla harassment against Royal Laotian positions.

Then came American involvement in Indochina. Again we could not fight the North Vietnamese on a football field with boundaries marked by fancy chalklines. The Viet Cong were using communication lines through Laos. The northern part of that country was literally riddled with Communist bivouacs—staging areas to move men and equipment south where Laos had a common border with South Vietnam. The Ho Chi Minh trail provided a handy little pipeline to safely transport guerrillas from north to south. That trail rambled through the mountain jungle of Laos.

Again we were forced to involve another sovereign nation in our military movements in Indochina. We began supporting and supplying the Royal Laotians.

Early in 1971 we launched a full-scale assault running up the Ho Chi Minh trail to intercept the Communist insurgents coming the other way. The operation was a success. We cleaned out thousands of Viet Cong and tons of ammunition. But just as the jungle closes up the burnt spot after lightning strikes a tree, so the VC came filtering back into the Ho Chi Minh trail. They could not be held back for long. Even though Laotian troops were positioned to stand guard after our withdrawal, the red tide was not blocked and our efforts were rendered ineffective.

As the Vietnam War ended, another cease-fire was signed in Laos, signaling the installation of yet one more coalition government and the ousting of all foreign troops. But the Laotian army would never be strong enough to make that mandate good, Communist insurgents would again move into military and political jurisdictions, and one more Indochina domino would topple.

CHAPTER 7

DOMINO FOUR
THAILAND

Thailand was never a part of the French Indochina we knew as was Vietnam, Cambodia, and Laos. In fact that ancient country, formerly called Siam, held the record in that part of the world for having never been taken over by any colonial power, though many tried. During the mid-1800s when the French and British were starting to throw their weight around Indochina, Siamese leaders signed trade agreements with those nations and became business partners instead of subjects of colonial Europe.

Although Thailand would appear to have a history of unity and concord, its internal problems were nonetheless typically Oriental after World War II. Major struggles occurred within that kingdom in the fifties and early sixties with one military coup after another.

Seeing the necessity for a friend in Southeast Asia we tried to stay one jump ahead, as the various governments came and went. We had been successful in bringing Thailand into SEATO in 1954, but due to her frequent changes in administration the tiny Asian country was never able to contribute a great deal to the defense pact. As the Indochina problem became more and more evident to us, however, we began to look for an ally. The closest one we could find geographically and politically was Thailand. We quickly entrenched ourselves in that country, building great airbases and naval posts. Several thousand Thai troops joined our GIs in battle, and by 1972 our strategists felt Thailand was our strongest ally in Southeast Asia. But Communist insurgency was ever present, especially in the northeastern section along the Laotian border. Terrorist raids became more and more frequent in the early 1970s.

Then came the end of the Vietnam War. As the U.S. pulled out of South Vietnam the Thais watched. They were unsure of their role. Would Saigon be able to hold out by itself? And if Thieu's government should fall, would the United States come to his aid?

These questions were answered in 1975 when the U.S. Congress cut off funds and the North Vietnamese overran Saigon. And as Thai leaders watched helpless South Vietnamese generals plead with the U.S. for assistance, their faith in us reached an all-time low.

What would prevent us from doing the same thing to Thailand? We could very easily build that nation up while the Communists regrouped, then walk out. What would be the disposition of Thailand then? Would our Congress suddenly negate the treaties once signed in good faith by our Department of State? The Thais wanted to believe in us, but we gave them little choice.

CHAPTER 8

NATIONALISM
OR COMMUNISM?

The most obvious symptoms of the problems in Indochina were military. We could see the guns and count the dead, but proper diagnosis would have told us that the disease we were trying to cure went far deeper than the militant surface. We tried to cure tuberculosis with mercurochrome. The deep-seated problems of Indochina were social and economic, and a solution would have required more acute insight into the Oriental psychology. Such analysis and treatment, however, would have been far more difficult to execute than simply unleashing our military power as we did on a trial and error basis.

I have never met an American I thought

completely understood the Oriental mind. And conversely I have never met an Asian who could comprehend in depth our Western thought processes. The two attitudes are diametrically opposed in many areas. Westerners have difficulty understanding the Orientals' qualification of trust, their insurance for loyalty, and their obsessive determination. The most obvious (yet quite complex) difference is perhaps the value systems of the East and the West. It is incomplete to say that Orientals place a lower value on human life than we do. Their sense of beauty in nature is more acute, and they have greater respect for esthetics than the average American. But their sensitivity to an individual personality within nature seems somewhat less than ours.

In Vietnam I witnessed peasants working and playing, enjoying their surroundings. No one seemed to have the ambition to rise above himself, but all took a common pride in the team. This need for unity appeared instinctive, but I'm sure it was nurtured by the difficulty a peasant would have in expressing individuality among mass humanity plus the longtime social system which discouraged rebels and promoted the "commune."

To inspire the average American sailor, I learned in leadership school, it is necessary for the officer to invoke one of two stimuli: either the promise of reward or the threat of punishment. Of course, that explanation of managerial prerogative oversimplifies the case. Still basic stimuli in Western psychology can be broken down to the satisfaction of goals achieved and the frustration of goals unachieved. And, knowing these basic mechanics of the American mind, military and political leaders as well as parents and teachers offer promises and make threats to achieve the desired response.

In Asia it seems to be a different ball game. To inspire the average Vietnamese to fight, one needs to offer more than promise of monetary reward, more than the prospect of personal freedom, and more than the insurance of big-brother support. And threatening him with "theory x" leads to little more success. Neither the threat of physical restriction nor a firing squad nor Communist domination seems to raise his brow.

During my imprisonment in North Vietnam I witnessed only two reactions on the part of the Vietnamese which I could logically attribute to a category of stimuli. Both were linked closely with survival.

The first response was daily when the cooks dished out the rice. There was never any doubt about a meal being taken for granted. It wasn't.

Like Pavlov's dogs, the peasants became genuinely excited when the chow bell rang.

The second type of response I observed was during the many air raids, but my observation time was limited. (Most of us were under our board beds praying for the accuracy of our comrades in the sky.) On one occasion, however, a conditioned reflex was readily apparent. It was movie day, and Gai Phong (Hanoi's answer to Warner Brothers) had outdone itself.

We sat on the floor in total darkness with armed guards at our elbows. The guards tried to play the role of unaffected jailers who were above it all. They made sure we maintained a good attitude (which meant we couldn't laugh at the MIG pilots or go to sleep on the floor). After the standard "shock" scenes of dead babies and bombed-out temples, the director turned his cameras to the cause of all the destruction. Three B-52s were pictured as their bomb bay doors were opened and scores of bombs slowly rippled from the bellies of the giants. That got attention.

The guards suddenly lost control of their facade and reacted naturally. Some gasped at the power. Others turned away, squinting. Still others became white-faced and open-mouthed.

In only these two cases did very primitive stimuli render a "standard" reaction. It was evident that our Western approach was too sophisticated. Just as the intensive indoctrination of the North Vietnamese to inspire American POWs to come over to the people's side fell on deaf ears, so did our psychology fail to bring the desired response from both friends and foes in Southeast Asia.

What *could* we have done? What action on our part would have stimulated our allies in South Vietnam to fight for what *we* believed in? Nothing short of a complete revamping of the social system with renewed emphasis on the society from the hamlet to the province to the national level could have turned the tide and given us the "hearts and minds" of the South Vietnamese people. And nothing short of unrestricted bombing of North Vietnam would have subdued Hanoi.

Communism? Capitalism? Socialism? None of these completely suit the people of Vietnam. Their brand of society is nationalism, and that nationalism must be an integral part of any social or economic order if it is to survive.

Our approach was the stick-and-carrot method. We offered the unpopular leaders great wealth and power if they would pass down the chain of command the vital enthusiasm we possessed for building a strong, free nation in Indochina. But the leaders didn't pass along the enthusiasm...or the millions. They put both in Swiss banks.

Had we stepped into South Vietnam with both feet, and from the very beginning demanded a restructured social order based on the historical needs of the people to be led at each level by dedicated citizens, then we could have offered a viable government acceptable to peasants, professors, and politicians alike. Only then could our brand of capitalism have meshed with their brand of nationalism to form an effective, legitimate government.

CHAPTER 9

FREEDOM
WITH DISCIPLINE

The single factor which tells the tale in battle and affects the outcome of armed conflict more than any other is discipline. We've seen that throughout history from Hannibal to Patton. When a leader can turn to his men, give an order, and know that it will be carried out to the letter, he has a powerful weapon. And his adversary with less discipline in his ranks has good reason to lose confidence.

But such a tool and such close-order drill by the very definition dictates a certain conditioned response from the rank and file. This blind following is mandatory within good discipline whether or not the soldier believes in the objective and rationale of his leaders. And therein lies a built-in problem. Discipline, if it is to be effective, must take precedence over personal freedoms.

Until the Vietnam War, the popular concept was that the average soldier was an obedient servant of his captain. No one wanted to see a soldier ordered into battle like a pawn in a game, but the act was condoned as "necessary for his country and for a good cause."

In the decade of Vietnam that faceless dogface suddenly became a personality, and that personality suddenly had basic human freedoms —more personal freedoms than any military man has ever had.

In our obsession to guarantee that every individual has the maximum possible freedom, we have forgotten the discipline required to insure and preserve that freedom. We are like the greedy fisherman who pulls in so many trout from the reservoir that none are left to spawn. If we cannot discipline ourselves against over-indulgence in freedom our great reservoir of liberty will be depleted.

The exploitation of freedom is a crime committed by all of us. No one is exempt from the responsibility to keep freedom alive. And in the military the problem of "freedom bloatation" does not end with the enlisted soldier; it goes right up the chain of command.

Each lieutenant wants to do his own thing and be a friend to his troops. Each colonel has certain ideas of his own and wants to be rewarded for his individual initiative. And every general prays for the chance to prove his strategy to Congress. At all levels private ambition takes precedence over duty to country. Again our system is self-defeating because of overemphasis on the very element which will destroy it—freedom of the individual.

How easy it must be to fight a war or run a government in a totalitarian state! What confidence it would give a military power or a civilian official to know he had the final say in every matter. And how nice it must be to completely control the press and thus the thought patterns of a questioning constituency. Every political and military leader in history has dreamed of such a utopia. But within the free world, none exists.

During the war, the greatest propaganda tool held by the North Vietnamese was our own division. Ironically, this was a product of our own personal freedoms—freedoms we were trying desperately to extend to our allies. The Communists watched closely all elected officials. Interrogators frequently spoke as if they were bosom buddies of "Bill" Fulbright and "Frank" Church. And with each change in U.S. voting record our captors would insure us that "another representative has seen the light and come over to the people's side."

As the war finally wound down, Congressmen were elected who were too young to have suffered a depression, to have fought in World War II, or to have experienced the value of good discipline. In their wonderful world of idealism, many set out to make everybody free. These new lawmakers seemed to believe they could legislate liberty with the swing of a gavel, that freedom should be reissued to those who abused it, and that discipline was old-fashioned and deserved to be ignored.

There is a thin line between freedom and discipline. We must be ever vigilant that one does not become the master of the other.

CHAPTER 10

THE
AUDACIOUS NORTH

"I just can't imagine how terrible that must have been," is a frequent reaction to my story as I travel about the country speaking and writing of my imprisonment. I find it impossible to make my audience know the emotions of a POW camp. I try, however, to psychologically transfer my listeners into the rags and filth of prison life. This is indeed a challenge. But the greater challenge in my attempt to make people understand Vietnam is describing the unbelievable naïveté of the North Vietnamese Communists.

Our captors acted like children in so many ways we were sure Gulliver's tale had come true and the Lilliputians had settled in Hanoi. They talked like children, sang like children, and even middle-aged military officers walked hand in hand like school girls. We could have easily accepted this apparent abnormality as a variation in culture (after all, we were a long way from home), but we found that these mature human beings *thought* like children too.

During one of my first weeks of imprisonment an enemy officer called me in for interrogation. The five-foot Vietnamese insisted that I sit on a small stool while he towered above me in his high-backed wooden chair. This ego trip I found to be the norm. After the initial round of questions he no doubt felt he had loosened my tongue. I had just been through a session with a guard we called Sadist in the torture chamber, and I was in fact loosening up a bit.

"What base you fly from?" he asked, taking a sophisticated puff from his home-rolled cigarette.

"*Kitty Hawk,*" I replied.

"*Kitty Hawk* is no base...is boat! I must know base."

I tried to be reasonable. "The *Kitty Hawk* is an aircraft carrier, and that is where I flew from."

"No," he became indignant, "I must know airplane base. Plane no can take off from boat. Aircraft need more zan two sowzan meter runway."

Realizing that we had more than a communication problem I decided to play his game. "You know we have many ships in the seventh fleet." He stared at me, trying to appear knowledgeable. "And many have top decks which are very flat." I paused for a reaction. Getting none I continued. "Well, we very carefully line up all those ships into one long chain and. . ." I stretched my arms in a one-that-got-away gesture. . . "we have a two thousand meter runway. We fly our planes from that."

And he believed it! In fact he thought I was devulging the secret of some new ultimate weapon.

One of the Communists' favorite stories was of a troop of "valiant freedom fighters" from a regional unit who had trained with painstaking skill a nest of hornets to do their dirty work. After several years of indoctrination, these winged soldiers could actually distinguish between capitalists and Communists and would, upon a prescribed signal, attack the former.

Several of the roving troups of performers reenacted a play depicting the Communist hornets. The Oriental music would drone as the puppet wasps on strings tied to bamboo poles would dance across the sky. Then, stage left, entered GI Joe. This character was always black-faced and sinister looking. The winged soldiers would attack (children were encouraged to cheer at this point), and the imperialist aggressor would be driven from the people's soil.

Their naïveté spread to the peace talks. There the enemy representative found it difficult to grasp the severity of the situation.

A short look back in history shows that when Communists came to the peace table they left their maturity at home. This was demonstrated by Khrushchev when he took off his shoe and pounded on the desk at the U.N. and again by the Chinese delegation at Panmunjom, Korea, when they sawed off the chair legs for all the American delegates. And following suit Le Duc Tho and Mm. Nguyen T. Binh approached the peace table with a modicum of maturity.

As Hanoi Hanna (North Vietnam's cheap copy of Tokyo Rose) broadcast the results of each weekly meeting at Paris, her American listeners (we had no choice) could almost mouth every word from memory. It was identical to the week before. She said the Paris delegation would first condemn the Americans for their "obdurate and perfidious" attitude and then renounce the U.S. representatives for trying to pull the wool over the eyes of the world.

In his excellent speech today, Minister Le Duc Tho proved once and for all that the American negotiations have been trying to confuse in the minds of the world's people the real identity of the aggressor and the victims of aggression. Being one nation from north to south, all Vietnamese have the right and responsibility of liberating all other Vietnamese. That is why the world is witnessing a great revolution from within the south parts of our country to free our people and throw the American aggressors back into the sea.

And that was the Communists' position. Never would they admit the obvious—that Hanoi had 150,000 or more uniformed troops and hundreds of thousands of guerrilla forces within the sovereign border of South Vietnam. Never would they respond directly to any peace initiative on the part of the U.S. delegation, but would instead reaffirm their self-appointed position of righteousness. It was tantamount to negotiating with a bamboo wall.

The Vietnamese had not really come to Paris "in search of a solution" to the war. They had come in search of a soapbox from which to inundate the Communist and free presses with their unbelievable audacity and their appeal for world sympathy. And it was obvious from the first few weeks that any serious negotiating would be done under, not on top of, the diamond-shaped table.

And so one more monkey wrench was tossed into the machinery of negotiation. It was the viewpoint of the audacious North.

CHAPTER 11

THE FICKLE AMERICAN PRESS

At sea a ship gets a reputation very quickly by the quality of the communications team it has aboard. As signals are sent by satellite or semaphore the skipper is very careful to watch "the traffic" for authenticity and clarity.

Between peoples a medium just as important yet seemingly uncontrolled carries ideas from corner to corner and continent to continent.

The fourth estate in this country is singly more powerful than any branch of government yet is controlled only by the interests of its owners. Singlehandedly the American press, it seems to me, acts as high court judge presiding in any area it desires jurisdiction. Abroad it acts as ambassador at large and serves to represent the United

States whenever and wherever the editors choose.

With the blessings of our founders, the American press was freed to respond to the people. And with an obsessive fear that this cornerstone of our Bill of Rights might ever be violated we have allowed it even more liberty.

The philosophy was outstanding. What could keep the leaders of this nation more honest and forthright than a faction of society insuring their constant visibility—an active public press? But in practice the philosophy of the free press fell short of its goal. The U.S. news media, intending to represent in some small way the viewpoint of its readership, often actually condemns and degrades much of what it examines, exposing only the negative side of the issue. And in doing this, it denies the constructive viewpoint it was designed to preserve. The disaster is twofold. In its negativism a large section of our press misrepresents America to our enemies. . . and to us.

The best propaganda pitch our captors had was the old ploy, "Your country has forgotten you," and they had plenty of newsprint to back up that statement. Front page headlines, complete with pictures and names, daily convinced the North Vietnamese that the U.S. was near collapse.

As I sat in the interrogation rooms of the "Hanoi Hilton" listening to a man who should have understood the American system I found it difficult to imagine how the backgrounds of two men could be so different that they derived completely diverse meanings from the daily news reports.

The leaders of that Communist country had grown up with a government-controlled press where little or nothing was ever said converse to any policy or individual. If it was about the government, it had to be good. If anything derogatory to the government ever appeared in that Communist press the readers could expect a shake-up, a major purge, or even a revolution.

On the other hand, we POWs had grown up with a built-in skepticism toward our press. We knew that the good news about our country was usually on the second page—in one column—if it appeared at all. And we learned to read the headlines not as facts but as the viewpoint of one advocate—the devil's.

Possibly the most frustrating feature of all was to watch our free press print stories in support of our enemy and then watch the Vietnamese leaders cling to the hope that the American people would soon rally into a militant force which would overthrow Washington and end the war.

We POWs weren't the only combatants

71

frustrated by the fickle American press. Our generals and admirals were equally distraught. Our free press frequently denied them a most important tool of strategy—the element of surprise. Our military positions, troop strength, and order of battle quickly arrived in Hanoi and Peking on AP, UPI, and Reuters. More frequently than we wanted to admit, our troops launched a "secret" assault only to find that the Viet Cong were waiting in ambush preempting our military movement. We sometimes blamed the tip-off on the South Vietnamese and the underground VC network. But more than once we found headlines for important operations going to print shortly after our soldiers mounted the helicopters.

The enemy, on the other hand, had complete media control. Nothing was ever said in *Nhan Dan* (Hanoi's daily) until well after the operation —and then only the aspects of the battle favorable to the Communists were presented.

During the war, American journalists were quick to point out U.S. mistakes and to condemn our involvement in Indochina. Each point was explored from every possible negative approach. A poll of editors in 1970 would have shown very few in support of the war and many in favor of immediate pullout. The exposure of our operations and strategy combined with the "big brother" influence of our press lengthened the war and made it unpopular at home.

Then the war ended. And while Americans sat back in relief the press continued to pick apart the methods by which the administration ended the war. But two years later when the dominoes of Indochina begin to fall, it began saying, "We didn't *fight* hard enough. We should have used our military power. We shudda' nuked 'em."

We repatriated POWs were the very few who had some immunity to the negative American media. As we stepped off those airplanes we were made heroes by TV and radio and the press—for a while. But the instant we opened our mouths and said something constructive about our country, they reacted. When we told how our faith in God and our deep love and commitment to our America helped us to survive, the media deemed it brainwashing. "The Commies tried to indoctrinate you for six years and couldn't do it. Now the CIA has done it in your two-hour flight to freedom. Who wrote your speech? Who told you to say that? Surely you can't mean those [positive] things!" We did mean those positive things and thanked God for our affirmative stance while we were in prison. Nothing could have been more destructive to our morale in that crisis than a negative attitude.

We were the biggest sensation since Chappaquiddick and no reporter could sleep without interviewing at least one POW. In the first two weeks I was interviewed nineteen times. And, as might be expected, I gained a certain insight into the techniques of stereotype reporters and a certain immunity to their audacity.

"The first hurdle is to gain rapport with your subject," I can hear the news editor telling his fledglings, "and when they get nice and comfortable...hit them with the hard stuff. That's when you get what you came for. That's when you get the sensational stuff."

In nearly every interview—TV, radio, or newspaper—I would be given a "typical example" of the questions to be asked. In some cases I would get a typed-out list of all the questions—well, all but a couple of impromptu ones—if time permitted.

The questioning would start innocuously with, "How does it feel to be home?" and "What did you miss most?" And just about the time I was beginning to enjoy the conversation I'd be asked, "How did you feel when you were napalming those babies?" or "What do you think of the turncoat wives who deserted you guys?" And what was edited to be shown on TV and printed in the papers? Generally the negative points of view.

This interview technique became so commonplace I frequently had to chuckle when a reporter gave me his list of "typical" questions. They were just like the last questionnaire.

The harassment didn't end as we slipped back into society. Nearly one year after our repatriation, the producer of a New York talk show called to ask me to participate in a "one year back home" look at the returnees. I told him I'd be happy to.

"We would like to explore some of the problems you have had in adjusting to normal life—you know, the horrible nightmares, the thoughts of revenge, and the attempts at suicide. The social withdrawal after the broken marriage."

"I'm sorry, sir," I responded in disgust, "but I have had no such problems. My adjustment has been the most wonderful experience of my life. I live and love every day with a positive outlook on everyone and everything—no nightmares, no suicides, no negative thoughts."

"Perhaps I have not made myself clear," he said and began to assure me that I could not possibly be normal if I didn't have at least some evidence of culture shock.

"I will be very happy to come to New York and

be on your program to tell your viewers of the exhilarating experience of a Rip Van Winkle who has found a rebirth of joy and happiness. But if your program is so distorted as to search out only the sensational, I cannot appear on it."

"In that case," he persisted, "could you give us the names of the MIA wives in your area who are still trying to adjust to life without their husbands?" With that I told him he was wasting my time and we terminated the conversation. The conversation had only added to my disgust with the media and their rape of the positive moral and religious values of this nation.

I know the importance of a controlled press to the leaders of Communist countries. I lived with censored news for six years, and I am adamant about having media in this country which can extol all sides of an argument and keep us all honest. But I fear that in its eagerness to "get the scoop" and be sensational our free press has shirked the responsibility which comes hand in hand with its powerful authority. It has forgotten to report the truth above all, and it has neglected to be positive.

I seek no government control of the media. It must be unrestricted in informing the general public the best way it can. But I would like to see more editors show more courtesy toward the positive viewpoint and give equal time to any agency of government wishing to rebut a charge.

"But positive stories won't sell papers," some editors tell me. I would challenge these editors and publishers to accept their responsibility of leadership in this country and print something worthwhile to guide readers rather than appease them.

Only with a healthy, competent news media can we stay informed on the issues of government. And only through this information can we make America a by-the-people nation.

CHAPTER 12

A NEW KIND OF WAR

Warfare, like nations, has evolved down through the ages, and historians would have great difficulty finding two wars or two nations with any great degree of similarity.

But just as West Point still studies Gettysburg and Annapolis follows Lord Nelson's skillful maneuvers, there is sufficient proof to indicate that the battlefield hasn't changed much from century to century.

There has been one innovation in the last few decades, however, with the introduction of electronics. Commanders can gather necessary information to make decisions and speed their decisions to the theater of combat for implementation. This drastic cutdown in lead time and reaction time has given much of warfare a new look. Sometimes the change hasn't seemed to be for the better.

In Vietnam we saw a much tighter command control from Washington and the Pentagon because satellites could beep telephone conversations around the world in microseconds. This rapid communication tended to remove a good deal of the authority from the on-scene commander whispering from his foxhole and place it with officials relaxing in plush offices thousands of miles from the bullets.

From a standpoint of coordination, this was usually advantageous. From a standpoint of command and control these absentee warlords tended to complicate the problem rather than solve it. Not only was the decision made without the full feel for the situation, but it was frequently made too late to be effective.

Frequent examples of this occurred as my squadron provided close air support for ground troops in South Vietnam. The forward air controllers could find the enemy, identify him, and mark him with flares, so that we could roll in before the VC got too close to the friendly troops. But because of our electronic hookup with Saigon and even Washington, permission had to be obtained from higher sources. The controller could only *request* the authority to fire.

In other words, the on-location commander could have made the decision and the job would have been done. But in this electronic war, our sophisticated communication system and the way we used it actually slowed us down until the target had disappeared or we were too close to friendlies to make a safe drop.

Another feature of our electronics was the speed at which the news got home. In every other war, mothers have anxiously awaited their sons' return or at least some information about them. In this one Mom could see her boy fight the "Reds" in living color. This brought the war painfully close to many households. But it brought new responsibility to our administration as well.

This daily "how goes it" was tantamount to an office memo from the administration to the American public asking for approval of military action for that day. So electronics may have actually held down atrocities like My Lai and Hamburg and the thousands of others that went without recognition in other wars.

Electronics gave us new ways to detect and destroy the enemy. This war brought snooper scopes and laser-guided bombs, mortar detectors and jamming devices that would make your fillings chatter. But for every new weapon we produced the enemy had a counter measure. It might be as simple as primitive camouflage...or as sophisticated as the most brilliant Russian engineers could produce. So, while technology had the ability to change the complexion of war, the determination of a people to win remained the deciding factor.

CHAPTER 13

MISTAKES
WE'VE MADE

In a sense there are no winners in war. Ticker tape parades and glistening medals symbolize the end of the conflict, but there are no real prizes—only consolation prizes.

The most important consolation we can take from the Vietnam War is the lesson we learned—a lesson which we hope will give us the knowledge and foresight never to let that happen again. After a war is an excellent time to take a close look at our government, our military, our foreign policy, and our motives. Just as surely as history repeats itself, we will make some of these same mistakes again. But with careful retrospect and closer discipline perhaps we can minimize the reoccurrence of most of them.

Our foreign aid program for the last decade has been in need of serious revamping. We try to assist poor people of the world, not in ways they want to be helped but in ways we think are best for them. Basic human dignity dictates that we should help a man help himself. In too many cases we have superimposed our methods and materials with little or no regard for the peasant and what he can do for himself. We have mail-ordered our dollars, our wheat, and our sophisticated machinery to the underdeveloped nations and expected them to react by sending heartfelt thanks to us—by return mail.

The machinery usually goes to the farms of the already wealthy landlords, the wheat goes to the black market, and the dollar goes in a numbered Swiss bank account. The heartfelt thanks are sent by the people who love us the most—and will desert us as soon as a better deal comes along.

We assume that what's good for us is good for our friends, and we go about the world imposing Boeing and Coca-Cola on small nations with the philosophy that "It made our country great and it will do the same for you." The error is that most of these struggling nations are not ready for planes and coke. They may need better rice strains and new wheels for the oxcarts; most are not ready or even interested in becoming great industrial powers. "We'll make them great whether they like it or not," is our attitude, and we proceed with great gusto.

The recipient countries often find our aid and our approach difficult to understand. These weren't what they wanted—or expected. But at least the dollars are pouring in. At least it will be good for the economy—maybe.

And as a tiny nation tries to adapt to a Western way of life, she falls farther and farther behind in this cultural-economic updating. The fancy John Deere can't make it through the jungle trails and gets bogged down in the rice paddy. No one can fix it when it breaks down. "And we're two weeks late with our planting."

The solution to this new problem is predictable —send the poor people some more money! And we do. But our added money combined with their confusion causes total dependence on America. They look to us at this point not only for dollars but direction.

They have lost their independence and their self-image as well. And that's where the whole system breaks down. When our friends lose their dignity they also lose their confidence in the United States. By this time their life-style is half tradition and half American, and they have nowhere to turn but to the second source of handout—Communism. And the dominoes keep falling.

The foreign aid scheme of the Communists is somewhat different from ours. They apply a more personal solution to the problems of their recipients. Russia is better able to send in advisers who will live with the poor and identify with their society. With this ability, the Soviets exact a higher price from a needy country. They require harsh discipline of the population and provide few real freedoms in return.

Foreign aid has been used as a tool of diplomacy for centuries. Having been helped in our infancy, we have passed along that goodwill to many others. But it works well only when the "attached strings" are combined with the true spirit of giving and sincere consideration.

In the 1960s and 1970s our assistance has not met the receivers needs. We have tried to use it as a political lever, and this has been a mistake.

Our second big mistake was imposing a half-hearted military solution to a socioeconomic problem. Some of the symptoms were indeed military, and we could not have survived a day in Vietnam without some armed force. But the disease was in the hearts and minds of the Vietnamese people, and we didn't offer any great antibiotic with our cokes or planes. Even so I believe more time could have been purchased with a stronger, less restricted military force. Had we followed a win strategy with our order of battle we could have stopped the infiltration and allowed the South Vietnamese the time they needed to establish a viable government.

In spite of all the strong points we can claim for our country, one of our short suits is choosing our friends. Had we chosen men who were already popular leaders or were even on their way up the ladder, we would have had a much better chance of appealing to the grass root masses of Indochina.

Perhaps the biggest mistake of all was allowing our national discipline to deteriorate. We did not resist the temptation to overindulge in freedom and thus lost the public and personal commitment needed to maintain our objective.

CHAPTER 14

CONSOLATIONS
OF THE WAR

Was our Vietnam experience in vain? We didn't achieve our original stated objectives. We failed to deliver the South Vietnamese from Communist bondage. We lost billions of dollars and tens of thousands of American lives. We even slipped a notch on the world's popularity poll. Even so, our involvement was not totally in vain.

The longer historians have to ponder the outcome of Vietnam, the more value they will see in our action there. Strategically, we brought many nations a good deal closer and made the world considerably safer during the decade of 1965-75 by our action in Indochina.

In the 1950s we temporarily stymied the spread of Communism in Korea by putting our foot down. But in the mid- and late-fifties the red cancer again began to spread—to Africa, to Asia, to South America. And just eighty miles from U.S. soil the international Communist movement infiltrated the small underdeveloped nation of Cuba. They bombarded that strife-torn, discontented country with their propaganda and agitations, and ZAP—it became part of the Communist block. They would have done that with great ease to all of Indochina if a succession of U. S. presidents hadn't said no.

We stepped in to bolster the first domino and were successful for ten years. We established a certain credibility in that decade by showing the world that the United States could sustain an unpopular war 10,000 miles away.

The Communists reacted. Within each of the individual governments a new respect for America was established. With that new respect—and possible fear—came new philosophies. The implementation of their peaceful coexistence policy was a direct result of our show of force in Vietnam.

While we POWs languished in prison, our commander in chief visited the two nations most actively supporting our enemy. We saw Nixon's tours of Peking and Moscow as evidence that the Vietnam policy was working, that détente could be brought about only from a strong political and military position, and that the only stimulus the Communists would respond to was brute force. We were showing them our muscle in Vietnam.

That decade can now be viewed as a time of delaying action to the toppling dominoes—an action which insured credibility and commanded respect from potential enemies. It also provided a great deal of experience. Our military was exercised. New weapons systems were developed and tested. Far better than in any other war, our statisticians with their complex computers were able to evaluate and reevaluate each new technique. We came home with a wealth of data concerning not only the hardware of warfare but the psychological problems and solutions too.

Soviet admirals and generals admit that the combat experience gained by American soldiers, sailors, and airmen will be a strong plus when they analyze our strength.

It was an expensive way to buy experience—and never would we have bargained to pay that price—but on the final tally sheet we can list that as a consolation.

As we prisoners sat out the war and wondered what was going on stateside our greatest disappointment was not the method by which the war was being fought or the anti-war element in our country but the apathetic American who chose not to think about war, anti-war, or much of anything else. Early in 1970 we evaluated our situation hypothetically. We estimated that 25 percent of all Americans thought we should be in Vietnam; 15 percent thought we should be out of Vietnam; and 60 percent were content to bring the Vietnam War into and out of their minds with a flip of a remote-control channel selector. Too many just didn't care.

"What the U. S. really needs," my cellmate would joke "is another Pearl Harbor, or a tidal wave to wipe out the West Coast, or a famine or fatal epidemic to shock people out of their lethargy." He wasn't serious about requesting a calamity, but in the dark ages of the late sixties something really was needed to get attention.

In 1970 the movement began. Americans came to life. With the POW movement and the war itself, citizens began to get involved.

After half a million troops and billions of dollars were sent to the East, Americans started to ask questions. And now that the episode is complete and we are finally awake we're still asking what happened. So perhaps the war did some good. It woke up a nation formerly content to sleep through rough times and wake up for the fun. It brought home to many the greatness of

America and how vital is its role as the guardian of freedom.

The lessons learned from Vietnam are far from finished. If we think back in future years to our mistakes we will find more and more guidance from reflection on our involvement in Indochina.

CHAPTER 15

THE LAST DOMINO?

The domino trick, played by children of all kinds, has few rules. All they need to do is to place each oblong piece in the correct position. Then, with a slight nudge of the first domino, they start a chain reaction that tumbles the whole row in less than a second. Then they're ready for another setup.

The political domino theory is neither as simple to explain nor as easy to reset as the child's game. While some aspects of it have been evidenced in Indochina, I believe that the problem goes deeper than most political analysts suspect.

For one thing, each domino is different. In Indochina, every country is made up of people with individual motives and desires. And while the Communists can set the stage to some extent, they do not have total power to adjust and readjust each domino in the lineup.

In a sense the domino theory has been proved, not by Communist acuity but by mistakes in our own foreign policy. Some of our errors have been easy to recognize in retrospect.

First we chose the wrong leaders. We assumed that any man with an allegiance to the U.S. dollar would have an automatic allegiance to his own country and serve the purposes of freedom.

Second, we tried to solve a political problem by buying time with restricted military power. When we found ourselves caught in the quagmire of a guerrilla war far from home, we refused to win. Even with our great military potential we refused to release the bonds of political restriction from our troops.

Our third error still exists. We are too free with our freedom. We are so obsessed with spreading it to everyone inside and outside the United States that we lose sight of its value and the price we paid to get it.

In these post-war years we must grasp every possible opportunity to reemphasize in the minds of every citizen the value of personal dedication to this society. We must revitalize our heritage of loyalty and pride. Only with the intense concern of all of us and with our active involvement in the policies of this government can we rise to achieve the heights worthy of our country's name—the United States of America.

The game of dominoes has no natural opponent. We have featured ourselves for many years not as players but as preventers of the game. And we take on the role of the great Colossus as we tower above the tiny wooden blocks, ready to intervene when one begins to fall against another.

We have a legitimate interest in the action and a perfect right to take part. The dominoes go around the world and represent real people "yearning to breathe free." But as the line stretches out of sight, Americans find more impetus for playing the game. The urgency comes as we consider the last domino. It could be marked U.S.A.